CW01267268

COURAGE OUT LOUD

WIDE EYED EDITIONS

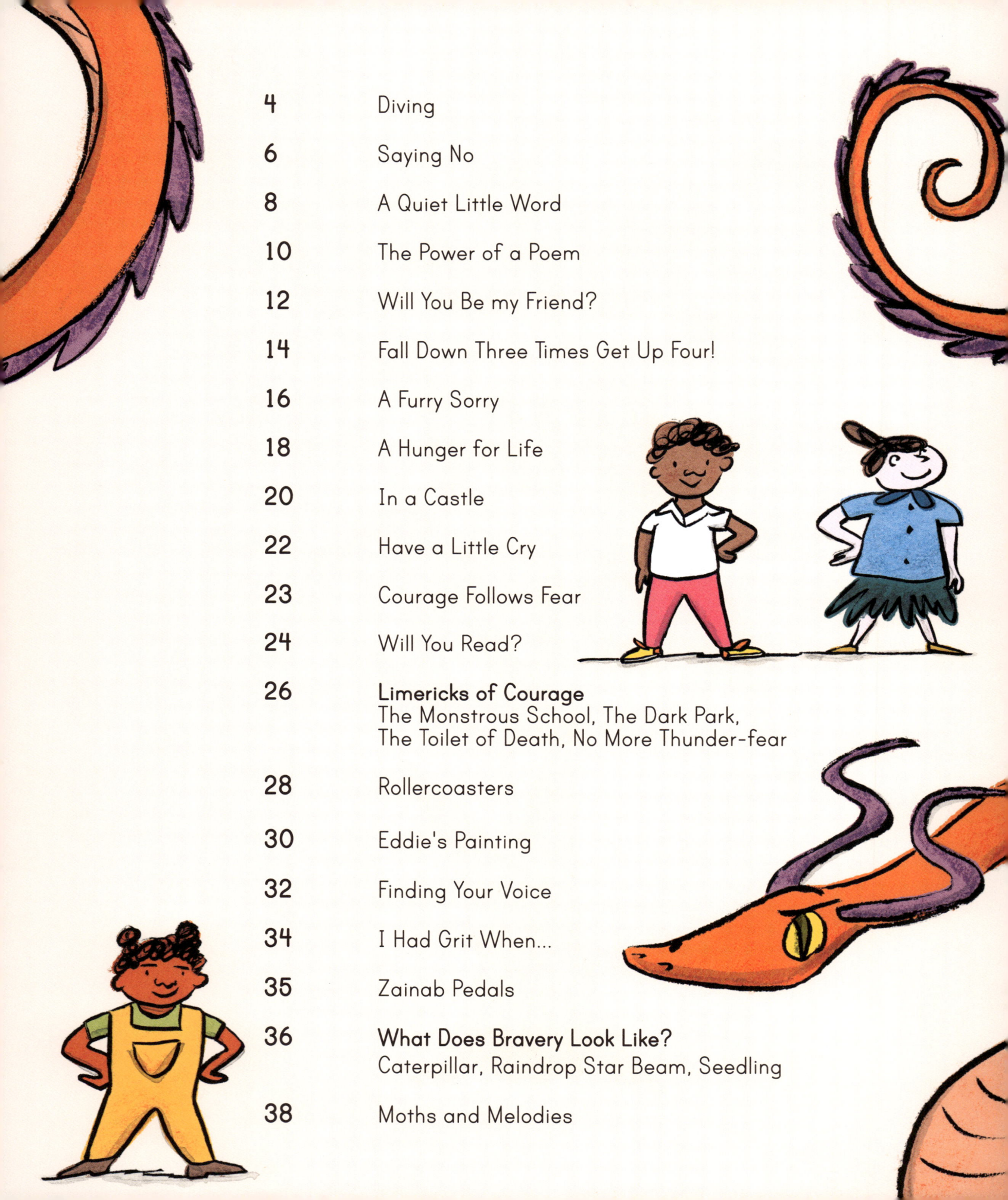

4	Diving
6	Saying No
8	A Quiet Little Word
10	The Power of a Poem
12	Will You Be my Friend?
14	Fall Down Three Times Get Up Four!
16	A Furry Sorry
18	A Hunger for Life
20	In a Castle
22	Have a Little Cry
23	Courage Follows Fear
24	Will You Read?
26	**Limericks of Courage** The Monstrous School, The Dark Park, The Toilet of Death, No More Thunder-fear
28	Rollercoasters
30	Eddie's Painting
32	Finding Your Voice
34	I Had Grit When...
35	Zainab Pedals
36	**What Does Bravery Look Like?** Caterpillar, Raindrop Star Beam, Seedling
38	Moths and Melodies

INTRODUCTION

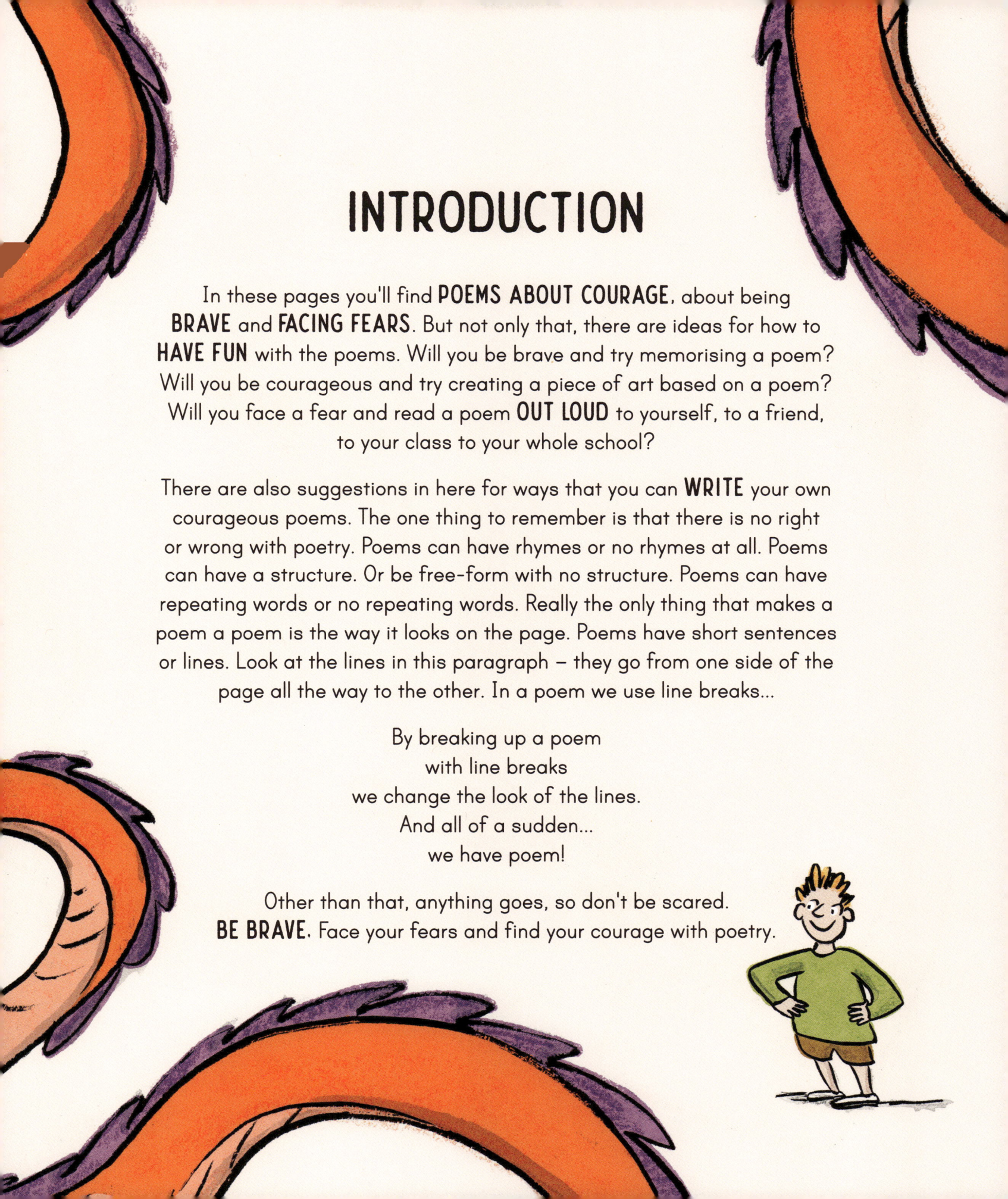

In these pages you'll find **POEMS ABOUT COURAGE**, about being **BRAVE** and **FACING FEARS**. But not only that, there are ideas for how to **HAVE FUN** with the poems. Will you be brave and try memorising a poem? Will you be courageous and try creating a piece of art based on a poem? Will you face a fear and read a poem **OUT LOUD** to yourself, to a friend, to your class to your whole school?

There are also suggestions in here for ways that you can **WRITE** your own courageous poems. The one thing to remember is that there is no right or wrong with poetry. Poems can have rhymes or no rhymes at all. Poems can have a structure. Or be free-form with no structure. Poems can have repeating words or no repeating words. Really the only thing that makes a poem a poem is the way it looks on the page. Poems have short sentences or lines. Look at the lines in this paragraph – they go from one side of the page all the way to the other. In a poem we use line breaks...

By breaking up a poem
with line breaks
we change the look of the lines.
And all of a sudden...
we have poem!

Other than that, anything goes, so don't be scared. **BE BRAVE.** Face your fears and find your courage with poetry.

DIVING

This poem is about the first time I faced a fear and jumped off a high diving board. I've linked that memory to some of my favourite fairytales. Can you have a go? Start with thinking of the fear. Was the thing you feared like a giant? When you faced your fear did you feel like Little Red Riding Hood? Ask a few more questions like this and you could have the start of a poem.

The diving board is up there,
a beanstalk above me,
a Rapunzel tower height,
a giant's hairline high.

I am scared but climbing,
pushing myself up the ladder
one rung at a time.
As the wolves in my tummy howl,
as the witches in my fingers itch,
as the trolls in my mind laugh.

The air feels thin,
the pool's sounds echo below me,
like the crunch of poisoned apples,
like the march of defeating armies,
like the rumbling of hungry ogres.

I creep to the diving board's edge,
the pool's sounds growl around me
and it feels like I'm...
pushing through a dark forest,
winding through a dark palace,
peering through a dark pool.

My friends are in the water below
laughing and smiling.
I close my eyes tight
as the pool's swirl roars,
and jump!

And I'm tumbling
down a rabbit hole,
rappelling down a hair rope,
falling into a well... **SPLASH**.

I kick and thrash to the surface
and I'm gasping and smiling
hugging and high-fiving my friends
and it's like...
we've got the magic beans,
we've stolen the golden egg,
we've just arrived at Grandma's house.

SAYING NO

It's great to try new things but sometimes we don't feel like doing something, and that's ok too. This poem uses a lot of rhyme. Can you write a rhyming poem about being asked to do lots of very silly things? Like putting jelly in your wellies! Or planting your socks! I'm guessing your answer would be to say "no"!

I would say "yes"
all the time.
"Yes" to this, "yes" to that.
I had a multitude of "yeses"
underneath my hat.

"Yes" to every question,
"yes" to things I did not want to do.
I had "yeses" in my pockets
and found "yeses" in my shoes.

"Yes" when I was tired,
"yes" when I was sad.
I would say "yes" to everything
even when "yes" made me feel bad.

"Yes" I can help you with your jacket,
"Yes" I can help you carry those.
But what is this beneath my feet?
A pile of little "nos".

"No" I don't want to go there,
"no" I don't want to play that,
"no" I don't *feel* like doing that thing
and that's the end of that.

I started to say "no",
never to be cruel or mean,
just when I didn't want to,
when I wasn't feeling keen.

Then a funny thing happened
when I decided to say "yes".
I said "yes" because I wanted to
and "yes" felt like the best.

I said "yes" and felt so happy,
I said "yes" and felt so strong.
I said "no" to playing football,
but said "yes" to singing a song.

I said "no thanks" to a hug
but "yes please" to a fist bump.
I said "sorry... no"
when asked if my skateboard
could be used for a skidding jump.

Now my pockets are full of "yeses"
but also quite a few "nos"!
I pick and choose between the two,
"yes" to these, but "no" to those.

"Yes" when I want to
or feel it's only fair.
"No" when I don't want to,
when there's something else
I'd rather dare...

Something else I want to try,
another thing I want to do.
So often a "no" to one thing
is a "yes" to something new.

A QUIET LITTLE WORD

Whenever I feel worried or scared about something, I find it helps to write about it. Sometimes I write a poem, sometimes a story. Sometimes I just write exactly what is worrying me. Next time you are worried, try writing a poem about it, it can rhyme like this poem, or have no rhyme at all. If you want to, you could even share it with someone special.

When fear and worry hound you,
and emotions are canned inside,
and no one understands you
and you want to run and hide.

When everything seems hard,
and you're feeling very sad
and life starts to bombard
with everything that's bad.

That's when a quiet word
can make everything better.
Release your worry-bird
in a poem, song or letter.

Uncage those barred-up fears,
watch them shrivel in the light.
Unbottle all those tears,
tell the world you don't feel right.

Speak to that special someone,
that someone who will listen.
Put down that worrisome tonne
and your joys will start to glisten.

It might seem a little scary
to share exactly what is real,
and you might be a little wary
to say everything you feel.

But with every little word
sung from your honest heart,
you will feel yourself stirred,
you'll feel brave, strong and smart.

And those tiny little words
will gather into a force –
a flock of mighty birds
that will set you on your course.

That will lift you out of fear,
take the worry from your head.
That will throw you like a spear,
shoot you like an arrowhead.

Have you whizzing through the clouds,
have you spiralling in the sky,
have you shouting to a crowd
that there's not a need to cry.

And then you'll be ready to hear
the tweet of another's worry-bird.
And give a little space to cheer
someone else's quiet, little word.

THE POWER OF A POEM

People sometimes are a bit scared of poetry...
that's because it's very powerful! Why not try performing
this poem with some friends? Divide the lines up between
you, read some lines separately, read some together. Maybe
you can get the audience to join in on the repeating lines.
Remember to smile and shout about the power of poetry.

A poem has the power
to build the highest tower,
to paint the prettiest flower!
A poem has the power.

In that tower of flowers
you may find a blooming power
as you paint with pollen and petal
you'll find a rose can test your mettle.

A poem has the skill
to cure any ill,
turn thoughts to windmills!
A poem has the skill.

As new ideas spin
the problems they're curing,
will waft away with time
all because of a little rhyme.

A poem has the capability
to conquer all hostility
to play a song of tranquillity!
A poem has the capability.

Words can hurt and soothe
but you'll make the spiky smooth,
apply a sentence like a balm
use a poem to heal and calm.

A poem has the might,
to give your passion bite,
to let your words take flight!
A poem has the might.

Your words might change a mind,
inspire someone to be kind,
or your words might roar
with the bite of a dinosaur.

WILL YOU BE MY FRIEND?

Think about the first time you met one of your friends. Where did you meet? Who spoke first? What was you first impression of them? What was the weather like? Have a go at writing a poem about the first time you met. It could be a long poem, or it could be short. It could have rhyme or no rhyme at all. Just remember to have fun.

What's harder
than climbing a mountain?
What's harder
than surfing a wave?
What's harder
than fighting a monster
or trying your best
to be brave?

It's telling someone you like them.
Telling someone
they remind you of you!
That out of all the people
you see everyday,
it is them
you want to stick to!

It's saying, "let's be friends."
"Let's laugh and joke together."
"Come rain or sweet breeze,
we'll be at ease,
no matter the roar of the weather."

It's easier than you think
to mould and form a new friend
just offer your hand,
let your heart expand,
and declare...
"This friendship won't end."

FALL DOWN THREE TIMES GET UP FOUR!

Think about an object (a prop) that could help you perform this poem. Could it be a hat? A walking stick? An umbrella? See what you have at home, and pick something you could imagine using in different ways during the performance – you could spin a hat on your finger, a walking stick could help you get up off the floor! Grab your prop and try performing the poem using the prop in different ways.

I'm feeling good, I'm walking tall,
I'm puffing out my chest.
I'm succeeding in everything,
I'm feeling my very best.

Until...
Oh no! I've fallen down.
I'm pressed upon the floor.
I've lost all hope, I'm giving up
I can't do this anymore.

But then...
My legs start to stir,
my hands and arms push up.
I find myself standing,
how did I ever think of giving up...

Until...
I've fallen on the floor again!
That's twice! What was I thinking?
I never should have tried to stand,
I've got that sinking feeling.

But then...
I turn onto my knees,
I crouch and then I lift,
I'm standing tall again,
standing is my gift...

Until...
I stumble, stagger, crash and fall,
the ground is rising up.
I won't be able to rise again,
I feel bad and fed-up.

But then...
my back begins to straighten,
I lift my head up high.
My head catching sunbeams again,
I let out a grateful sigh.

Standing is getting easier,
I'm stronger than before,
and because of all my floundering
I no longer fear the floor!

I'll fumble and I'll falter, I'll wobble and I'll lurch,
on some days I'll slither, on other days I'll perch!
Life is a journey, a never-ending search.
I'll always try to stand! Standing is my church.

And when I'm next on the ground
my failures scattered all around.
I'll plaster my wounds and caress every bruise,
I'll look up from the ground at a brilliant view.

I'll look up to the heights that abound overhead
and tie up my failures with a gold-silken thread.
With my head in the clouds and my feet on the land,
I'll gather up every lesson, and again I'll stand.

A FURRY SORRY

Draw your very own furry sorry. What does it look like? Does it
have two legs? Four legs? Six legs? Is it like a cat, or a puppy?
Does it look like a kangaroo? What colour is your furry sorry?
Let your imagination run wild.

I did something wrong.
I know I should say sorry
but there's a wall in my mouth,
there are chains around my teeth
and an ache in my heart.

The wrong I did
seemed small at the time,
it rolled out of me
unthinking.

As soon as I saw it,
I knew,
but it was too late.
A space within
filled up with shame
and the need to be right.

So I pushed the wrong further,
gave it a kick
and watched it cascade
over those I love.

I did something wrong.
I know I should say sorry
but my throat is a mountain
and my sorry feels so small.

Then I see the hurt
in the eyes of those I love,
and my little sorry starts to climb
from the well of my stomach.
Starts to move its small furry arms
past the crags of shame and guilt in my chest.

The sorry is small
but it is strong!
It leaps the wall of my mouth,
breaks the chains of my teeth,
and heals the ache in my heart.

A HUNGER FOR LIFE

Try reading this poem using lots of actions. Pretend to try each type of food and use your face to show how it tastes. Will you scrunch up your face? Will you stick out your tongue? Will you smile and lick your lips and rub your tummy?

I don't eat green things,
weird things or mauve things.
I don't eat spiky things,
mushy things or spicy things.

The market stall was heaving
with things strange and quivering.
Mushy things, squashy things
bright and odd-looking things.

"Try these legs of a roofolian dog-spider",
said the market trader with a grin.
"Fried in gelatinous beetle fat,
these beauties are just in!"

"Or how about these hairy wings
cut from a pig-dandelion's back?
These delicacies are just the thing
to have you constantly coming back."

"No thank you", I murmured.
"Weird things are not for me,
I don't like to eat anything
that can't be paired with a cup of tea."

The market trader smiled gently
and reached into a bag
he pulled out something nasty
wrapped up in a fraying rag.

"I have just the thing
for someone afraid of the new
it's the very essence of courage,
it's the perfect thing for you."

His hand shot suddenly upward,
pushed something yucky into my mouth.
It slipped right down my throat –
a slimy mass heading south.

I wanted to yell and vomit,
to rant, rave and throw up,
but a sudden warmth in my belly
refilled my courage cup.

A sudden joy found my lips
as saliva swished my gums.
The stall looked like a funfair,
a paragon of fun.

The stall-holder offered up sticks
with lumps skewered on the ends
and from an odd upturned decanter
a thick liquid started to descend.

I grabbed and slobbered and swallowed,
passed every oddity over my tongue.
I gnashed and gnawed and nibbled
every item the stall-holder flung.

Every gulp offered delight
both disgusting and sweet,
every taste a new experience
as I found a new way to eat.

A new courage for food
started to swell, started to expand.
I felt I had bravery
curled up in the palm of my hand.

I hungered for adventure,
felt a thirst to try new things,
found I could digest a new life
just from a simple change in dining.

IN A CASTLE

This type of poem is called a sestina. Sestinas use the same six ending words in each verse but in a different pattern each time. This sestina tells a story. Copy out the poem one verse at a time and draw a picture for each one, showing the little knight and the dragon and their adventure together.

In a castle on a hill lived a little **knight**
reading many wondrous books in her little **fort**.
She read her books by candle**light**,
she read of forests where secrets **blew**,
where swashy squalls would splash and **groan**
among the waves of the cave-cliff **sea**.

She dangled a rope down to the **sea**,
down to the boat that big **knights**
row when they are big and fully **grown**
with armour wrapped in midnight **blue**
she weaved the maze that hid her **fort**
and rode out into a world of **moonlight**.

She followed fluttering swarms through the luna **light**.
Sword in hand she hacked a path to **see**
the ponds where the frogs glow **blue**.
As the stars gasped in the sky's delighted **night**,
her head was filled with many delighted **thoughts**,
until she heard a bellowing **GROAN**.

It was a deep and dreadful **groan**,
loud enough to silence star**light**.
Her head filled with many dreaded **thoughts**
as the swashy squalls thundered by the cave-cliff **sea**,
as the blazing frogs croaked in the fear-soaked **night**,
as the dragon's orange flame burned **blue**.

Armour wrapped in midnight **blue**,
she felt the fear of those known to be **grown**.
She could not run. "I AM A **KNIGHT**!"
She faced the dragon's blue burning **light**.
She swished her sword so the dragon could **see**
that a battle of shield and wing would be **fought**.

They swished and flapped back to the **fort**,
as the night drained from black to **blue**.
The dragon stopped, stunned to **see**
a fort full of books – where the shelves did **groan**.
His tail swished, a book landed, bathed in **candlelight**...
A picture of a dragon and a **knight**.

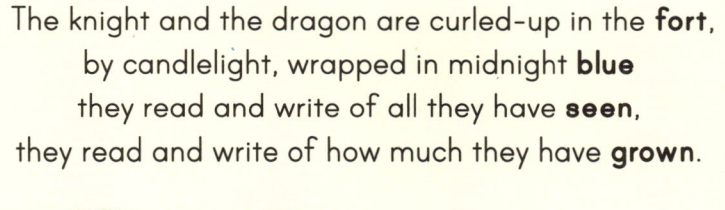

The knight and the dragon are curled-up in the **fort**,
by candlelight, wrapped in midnight **blue**
they read and write of all they have **seen**,
they read and write of how much they have **grown**.

HAVE A LITTLE CRY

Everyone cries sometimes. It can really help you feel a bit better. Why not try memorising this poem so that next time you have a little cry you can remember that there is courage in every tear.

When night feels too long,
when every breath is a quivering sigh,
when your heart can't hear its song
and clouds steal the stars from the sky.

That's when your courage ignites,
you'll feel it tingling behind each eye,
not the courage to shout or fight
but the courage to have a little cry.

To let the tears fall
no matter who might hear,
take a deep breath and bawl —
there is courage in every tear.

COURAGE FOLLOWS FEAR

This type of poem is called a rondel it repeats some lines in the poem. Copy out the poem and highlight the repeating lines, discover where they are in the poem. Can you write a similar poem with repeating lines too?

Courage is the fire that follows fear's smoke
there must be fear for courage to alight.
Braving the dark while fearing the night.
It's not courage if you yearn for night's cloak.

Welcome the shake and stutter, the flail and choke,
they sing the coming of new-born might.
Courage is the fire that follows fear's smoke.
There must be fear for courage to alight.

Courage is action despite fear's warning croak –
the surprise of a nervous warrior's fight,
the fearful attack of a hounded prey's bite,
the sap that seeps when an axe bites your oak.

Courage is the fire that follows fear's smoke.

WILL YOU READ?

When practising reading poetry out loud one of the best things you can do is read the poem again and again. Each time you do, try putting emphasis on different words. Try changing your voice, can you do a different voice for Sir? Try putting different emotions in your voice. When you find your favourite way to read the poem, try being brave and reading it to someone else.

"Will you read your story
to the class?"

Sir's question comes like a lightning strike.
I'm scared to do it
but I am standing.

The classroom is a swamp,
mud oozing around my legs.
The only way out is forward.

School desks erupt around me.
I hop the lava of the students' stare.
The only way out is through.

Tonya Smith is a giant.
She looms over me, she booms over me
and birds are blown from the trees.

I edge to the precipice
of my tumbling stomach,
balance the skittles
of my trembling knees,
climb the heat
of my flushed face
to the very peak of the class.

"Are you ready?"
Asks Sir.

I take a deep breath
and I read.

25

LIMERICKS OF COURAGE

Limericks are traditionally read to make people laugh. Practice reading these poems to yourself. When you feel happy with how you read them, have a go at reading them to a friend. Can you make them laugh?

THE MONSTROUS SCHOOL

There was a young child from Poole
who was terribly scared of his school.
"There's nothing to fear" said the head
but the poor lad felt such dread
when he saw the school gates start to drool!

THE DARK PARK

Young Sabina was scared of the park
with its branches all pointed and stark.
She decided for fun
to conquer her fear in a run
but was swallowed at once by the dark!

THE TOILET OF DEATH

Little Laila visited the loo
where she had heard of a monstrous poo.
She intended to flush
with a plunger and brush
but alas, she was flushed down too!

NO MORE THUNDER-FEAR

"No more will I fear the thunder!"
Said Karina as the sky tore asunder.
She climbed up the highest hill
and felt the rain's deadly chill
then was struck and sent six-feet under!

ROLLERCOASTERS

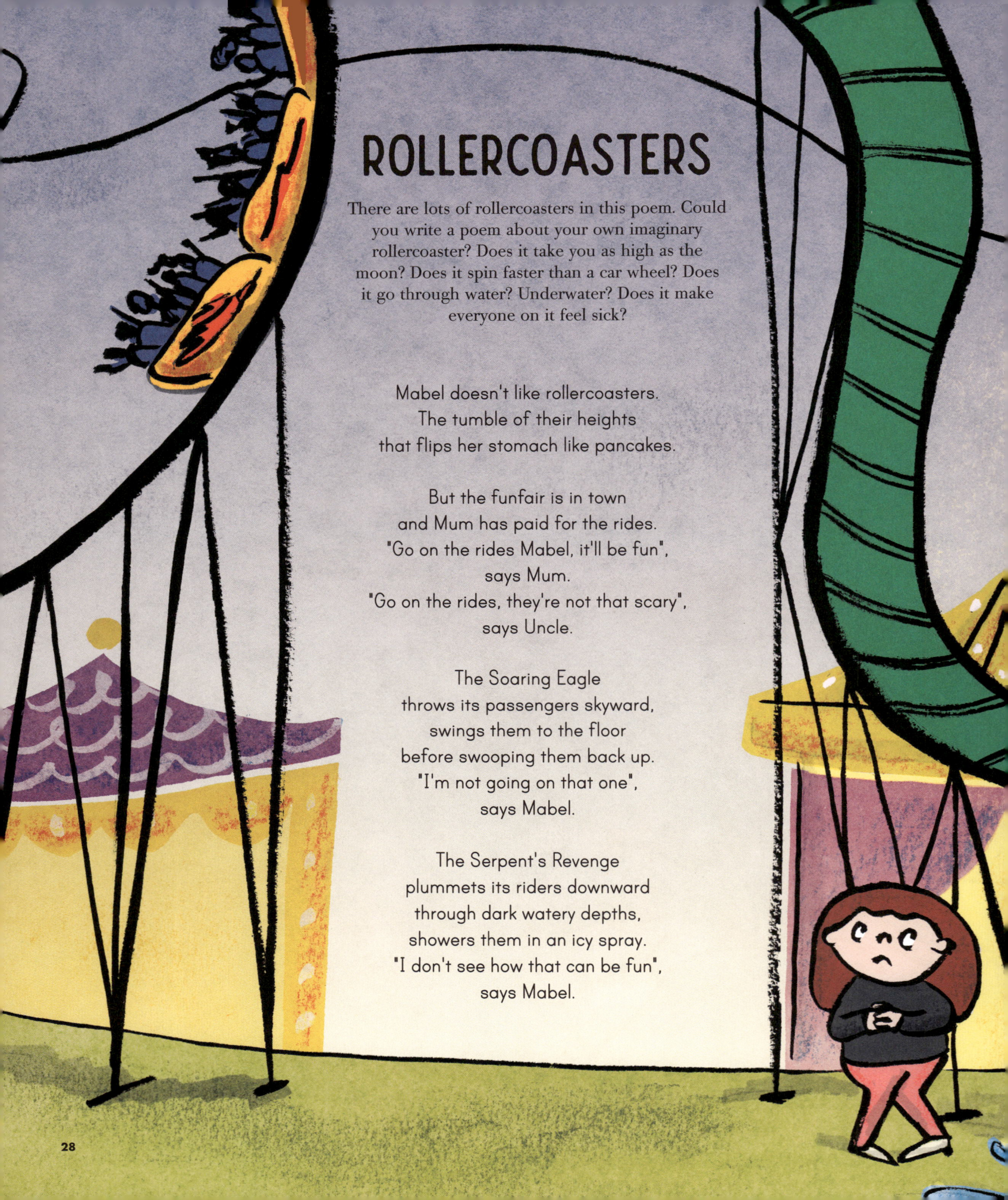

There are lots of rollercoasters in this poem. Could you write a poem about your own imaginary rollercoaster? Does it take you as high as the moon? Does it spin faster than a car wheel? Does it go through water? Underwater? Does it make everyone on it feel sick?

Mabel doesn't like rollercoasters.
The tumble of their heights
that flips her stomach like pancakes.

But the funfair is in town
and Mum has paid for the rides.
"Go on the rides Mabel, it'll be fun",
says Mum.
"Go on the rides, they're not that scary",
says Uncle.

The Soaring Eagle
throws its passengers skyward,
swings them to the floor
before swooping them back up.
"I'm not going on that one",
says Mabel.

The Serpent's Revenge
plummets its riders downward
through dark watery depths,
showers them in an icy spray.
"I don't see how that can be fun",
says Mabel.

But the Party House looks ok
with smiling clown and signs that declare,
"Fun for all the family."

"Maybe I'll give this one a go," says Mabel.
Mabel, Mum and Uncle queue
and queue and queue.

Inside is dark,
music is playing
sweet smells fill the air.
"Are you ready for the party?",
grin the clowns.

Mabel, Mum and Uncle
climb into their seats
in a big room.
It looks like a banquet for giants.
"I wonder why they need harnesses?",
asks Mabel as the Party House ride begins.

The lights dim,
the music blares
and the seats start to move,
start to tip!
The banquet table tips too,
the whole room starts to spin.

"I don't like it", says Uncle.
"I want to get off", says Mum.
"This is brilliant!", says Mabel.

EDDIE'S PAINTING

Can you recreate Eddie's painting? Remember it's ok to do lots of versions and to pick the one you like – that's part of the fun. Don't worry if you don't have paints, you can draw it with pencils, or crayons or felt-tips instead.

Eddie's first painting
was no good.
The people were all splodges
and the sky had run.

Eddie's second painting
was no good.
The trees looked odd
and the buildings were wonky
but the sky looked marble!

Eddie's third painting
was no good.
He had tried to paint his dog –
it looked more like a cat.
But the trees looked alive.

Eddie's fourth, fifth,
sixth and seventh paintings
were no good.
The colours were all wrong,
the brushstrokes were messy,
but when he looked at it,
he looked through it.

Eddie's eighth painting
won a prize!
It had marble skies,
and living trees
and splodges of people
that spoke of life and living and art.

31

FINDING YOUR VOICE

If you were looking for your voice, where do you think you would find it? Would it be under a waterfall in a jungle? Would you have to travel deep under the sea in a submarine? would you have to take a rocket to Mars? Write a poem that tells the story of your search for your voice.

Sit very still
in a quiet room.
Listen to your breath
and search inside.
Listen for the ebb and flow
of your voice.

Sieve imaginary hands
through the sands
of your beliefs.
Your voice is in the warmth
of those shifting dunes.

Look to the sky
of your happiest memory.
Your voice is in the exhale
of that endlessness.

Hold the concern
for the ones you love.
Your voice is what nestles against them.

Feel the solidity of your body
the weight of your bones,
the love in your heart.
Your voice moves through each one
in every part.

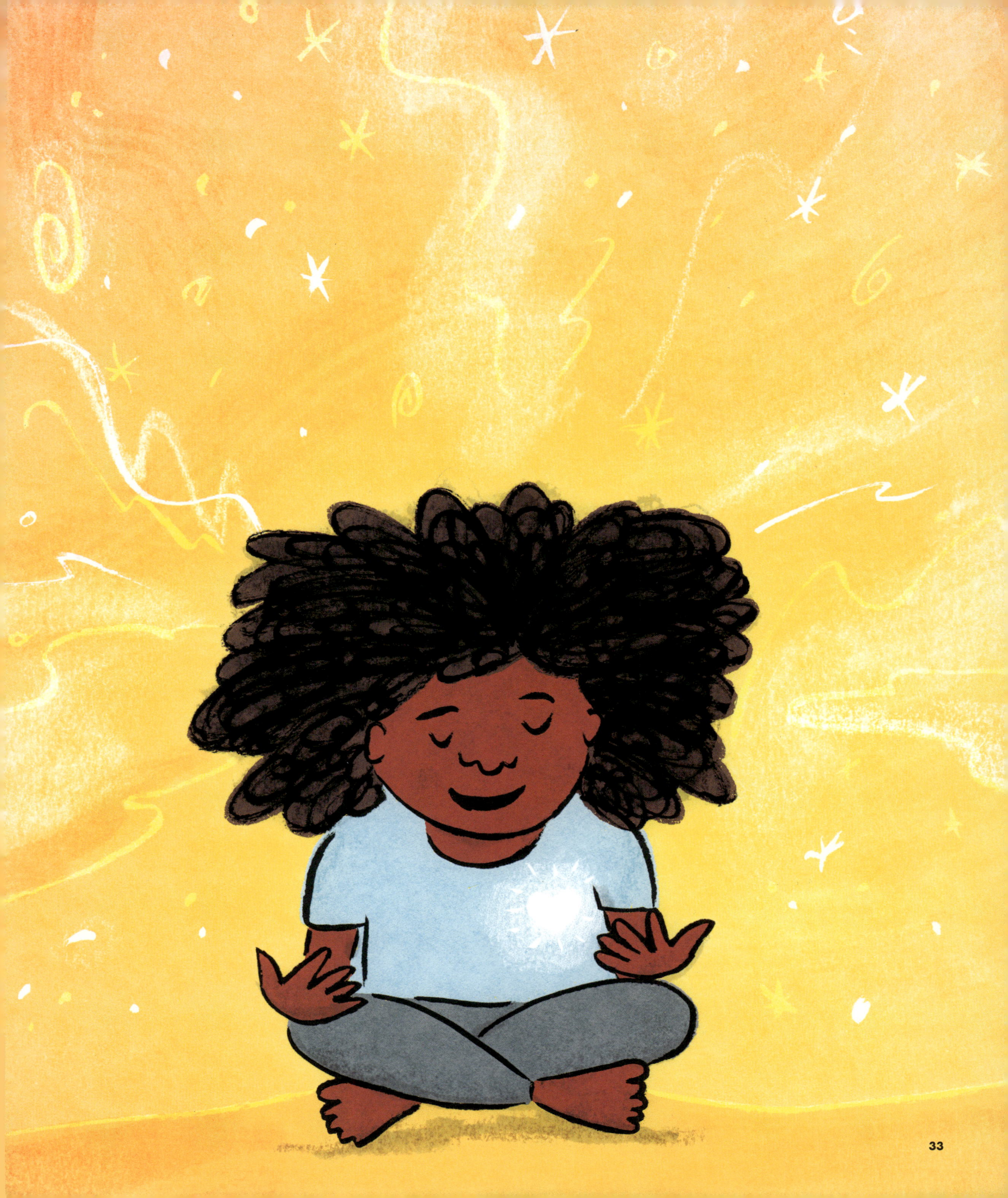

I HAD GRIT WHEN...

For the first verse of this poem, I simply thought of some times I was brave and listed them. For the second verse I listed what happened next. For this verse I tried to use interesting words to make the poem 'pop'. Have a go at writing a poem about the times you have had grit!

I got on the plane for the first time,
took two steps towards her shouts,
boarded the bus at midnight,
spoke my words into an envelope,
uploaded my needs to an email,
cried tears into their ears.

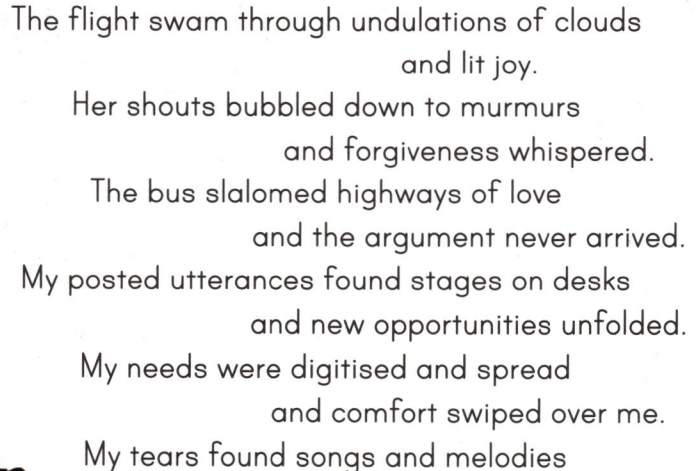

The flight swam through undulations of clouds
    and lit joy.
Her shouts bubbled down to murmurs
    and forgiveness whispered.
The bus slalomed highways of love
    and the argument never arrived.
My posted utterances found stages on desks
    and new opportunities unfolded.
My needs were digitised and spread
    and comfort swiped over me.
My tears found songs and melodies
    that my family and I sang together.

ZAINAB PEDALS

This type of poem is called a pantoum – in each verse some lines repeat and some new lines are added. Draw lines between the lines that repeat – see if you can work out the pattern of the poem. Try making the poem your own. You could change the name of the character or have them swim in a pool instead of pedalling a bike. But be careful if you change the end words, the rhymes will have to change too!

Zainab looks up and starts to pedal
the hill is steep, will she reach the top?
She entered this race desperate for a medal,
now the fear sinks that she might have to stop.

The hill is steep, will she reach the top?
Cyclists pass as her legs start to burn.
Now the fear sinks that she might have to stop,
the road behind her whispers "return".

Cyclists pass as her legs start to burn,
she wipes her brow, breathes the air deep,
the road behind her whispers "return".
She shuts out the noise, new strength starts to seep.

She wipes her brow, breathes the air deep,
feels the fear within quickly fall apart.
She shuts out the noise, new strength starts to seep,
feels the gold of her lungs and her heart.

Feels the fear within quickly fall apart,
she entered this race desperate for a medal,
feels the gold of her lungs and her heart.
Zainab looks up and starts to pedal.

WHAT DOES BRAVERY LOOK LIKE?

What do you think bravery looks like? Write a little poem about unusual things being brave. To start with, try... a rainbow, a flower, a mouse and an apple. How would these things be brave?

CATERPILLAR

A brave caterpillar spins a cocoon, not knowing what it will become but dreaming of flight.

RAINDROP

A brave raindrop falls, aware of the ground below, knowing the sun will lift her.

STAR BEAM

A brave star beam journeys into space,
ignorant of eyes and telescopes
but wishing to marvel.

SEEDLING

A brave seedling unfurls
in concrete crack and crumbling wall,
oblivious to sunlight and rainfall
but trusting in growth.

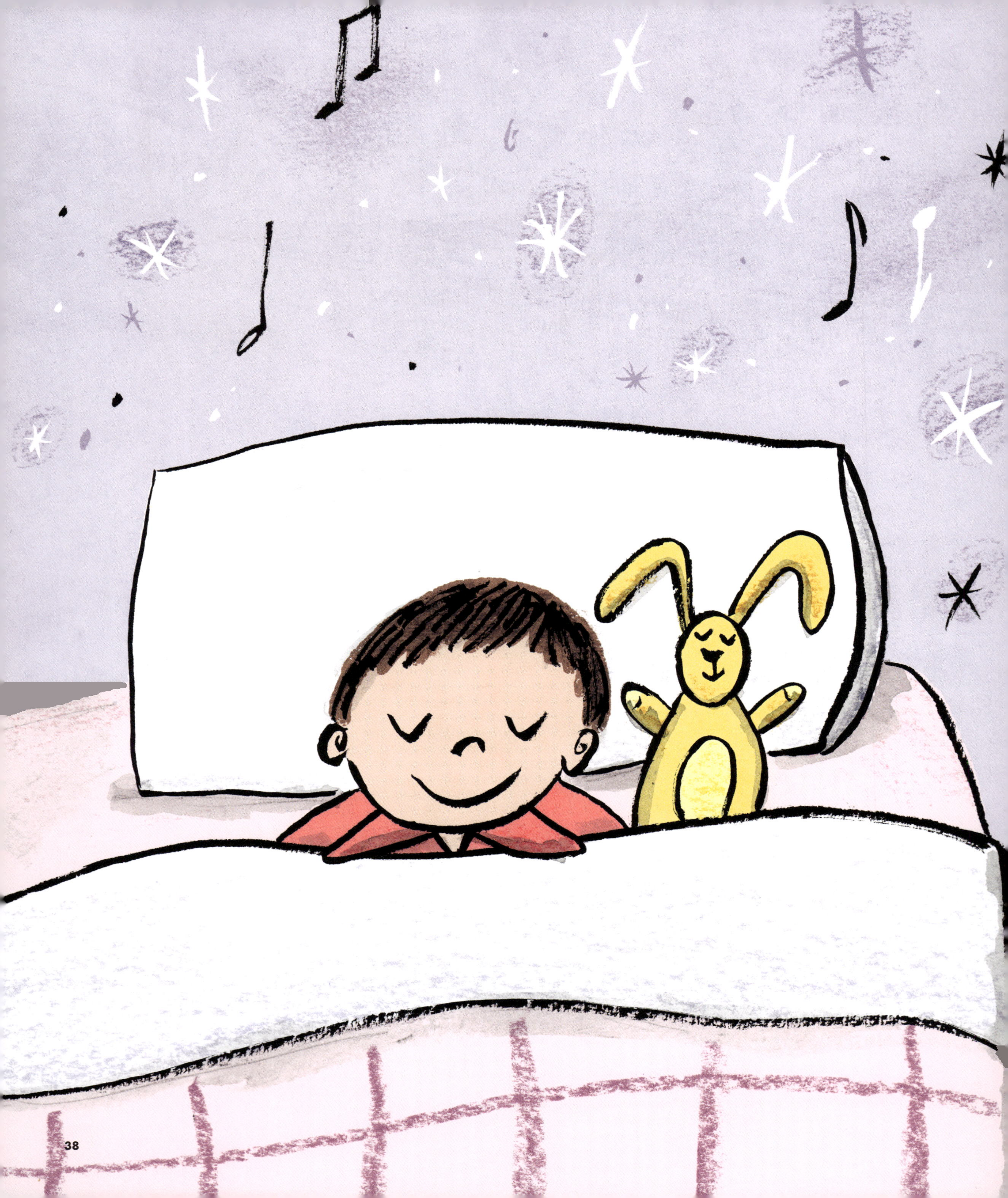

MOTHS AND MELODIES

This type of poem is a ballad. It uses rhyme and has a relaxing rhythm. Practice reading this poem emphasising the rhyme and the rhythm, see if you can learn it off by heart, and maybe read it to a family member before bedtime.

As nighttime's fingers itch and reach
and tug upon my cover,
I try to imagine I'm on the beach.
It's no use, I call for mother.

"No need to fear the dark", she says.
"Without the dark there'd be no stars."
"Nighttime lifts the moths wing", she says,
"and holds music in a guitar."

I dream of moths and melodies
of stars hugged by a blanket dark,
mother's words – just the remedy,
they shine a comfort into my heart.

Courage is not the absence of fear, it is striving forward despite the fear you feel. This book is for all of those who feel afraid. You need to feel fear if you are to be courageous. May these poems help you take that first brave step. – J.C.

For DB, for helping me find my own courage. – D.G-B.

Courage Out Loud © 2023 Quarto Publishing plc.
Text © 2023 Joseph Coelho.
Illustrations © 2023 Daniel Gray-Barnett.

First published in 2023 by Wide Eyed Editions, an imprint of The Quarto Group.
One Triptych Place, London, SE1 9SH, United Kingdom.
T (0)20 7700 6700 F (0)20 7700 8066 www.Quarto.com

The right of Daniel Gray-Barnett to be identified as the illustrator and Joseph Coelho to be identified as the author of this work has been asserted by them in accordance with the Copyright, Designs and Patents Act, 1988 (United Kingdom).

All rights reserved.

No part of this publication may be reproduced, stored in a retrieval system, or transmitted, in any form, or by any means, electrical, mechanical, photocopying, recording or otherwise without the prior written permission of the publisher or a licence permitting restricted copying.

A catalogue record for this book is available from the British Library.

ISBN 978-0-7112-7919-3
eISBN 978-0-7112-7922-3

The illustrations were created with traditional and digital media
Set in Nature Spirit, Bodoni and Print Clearly

Published by Debbie Foy
Designed by Myrto Dimitrakoulia
Commissioned and edited by Lucy Brownridge
Production by Dawn Cameron

Manufactured in Lithuania BLT052023
9 8 7 6 5 4 3 2